DARE to ASK

2701367

DARE *to* ASK

Call to Me, and I will answer you, and show you great and mighty things, which you do not know.

— Jeremiah 33:3 NKJV

Equipping Leaders. Spreading the Gospel. The International Leadership Institute changes history by accelerating the spread of the Gospel through leaders empowered by the Holy Spirit. The Gospel saves, redeems, delivers, transforms, and restores. Jesus is our only hope.

Dare to Ask is an inspiring collection of stories and vivid images from men and women who put their trust in God and dared to ask Him to use them. Over and over again, these leaders took significant risks as they earnestly sought God, and He was faithful to honor their cry. Walk by faith. Live boldly. Dare to ask. Experience His presence and power.

We hope these stories will encourage, challenge, and inspire you to ask God for great and mighty things. God promises He will answer.

Until all worship,

[signature]

Wes and Joy Griffin
International Directors

ILI is a global movement of faithful men and women who are passionate to change history by training and mobilizing leaders of leaders to reach people with the power of the Gospel of Jesus Christ. Each year, more than 500 leadership conferences equip men and women around the world with the Eight Core Values of the most effective Christian leaders who are fulfilling the Great Commission to "go and make disciples of all nations."

GET
CONNECTED

ILI TEAM APP

The new ILI Team app is your connection to the ILI Team around the world. Access resources, social media, blogs, testimonies, online giving, and more. You can also connect with the ILI office, submit prayer needs, and check out the global training calendar.

ILITeam.org/app

ATTEND A CONFERENCE

With more than 500 conferences each year, there is a training event for you! Attend an ILI National, Regional, or History Makers Conference and be equipped with the Eight Core Values of the most effective Christian leaders.

INTERNATIONAL LEADERSHIP INSTITUTE
equipping leaders. spreading the gospel.

ILITeam.org/calendar

BLOG AND PODCAST

Did you know ILI produces blogs and podcasts filled with leadership principles and inspirational lessons? Subscribe today!

ILICoreLeadership.org
ILITeamTalk.com

MORE FROM ILI

Want more from the ILI Global Team? Check out our Connect page to read testimonies, download ILI magazines, follow our social media pages, submit prayer needs, and more!

ILITeam.org/connect

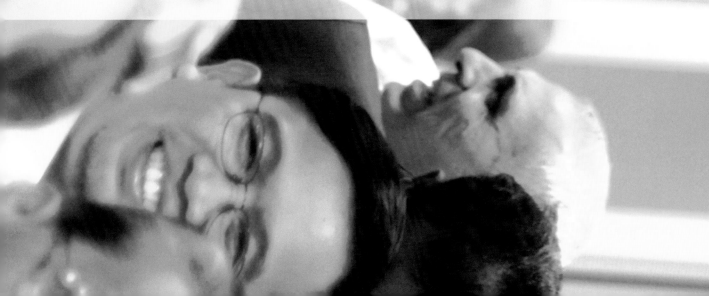

100 NATIONS INITIATIVE

At the 2015 Global Summit, God gave the ILI leaders a vision to see teams equipping leaders and spreading the Gospel in at least 100 nations by 2020. When Jesus said, "Go and make disciples of all nations," He was instructing His followers to join His mission and reach the world with the Good News.

With each new advance, a deeper prayer commitment is required. This is why we created the "Dare to Ask" prayer campaign. Each week, we focus our prayers on two nations and include a brief update on the status of the Gospel in those locations. This prayer focus is shared through email and social media every Monday in English, French, Spanish, and Portuguese, with plans to add more languages. Sign up to receive the weekly "Dare to Ask" email or follow the ILI Team on social media.

ILITeam.org/daretoask | ILITeam.org/connect

One priority of the 100 Nations Initiative is countries where Christians are routinely persecuted and the Gospel is least accessible. For security purposes, ILI's work in these nations is not publicized. Plans are in place to expand the ILI training to as many distinct people groups as possible within each nation. Teams are diligently working to extend their reach—the India team plans to impact 10 new language groups this year, the Myanmar team has identified 37 language groups to be reached, and in the USA, ILI training is available in English and Spanish, with dreams of reaching more languages in the near future.

Check out video updates on the 100 Nations Initiative from ILI global leaders at ILITeam.org/100nations.

CONTENT

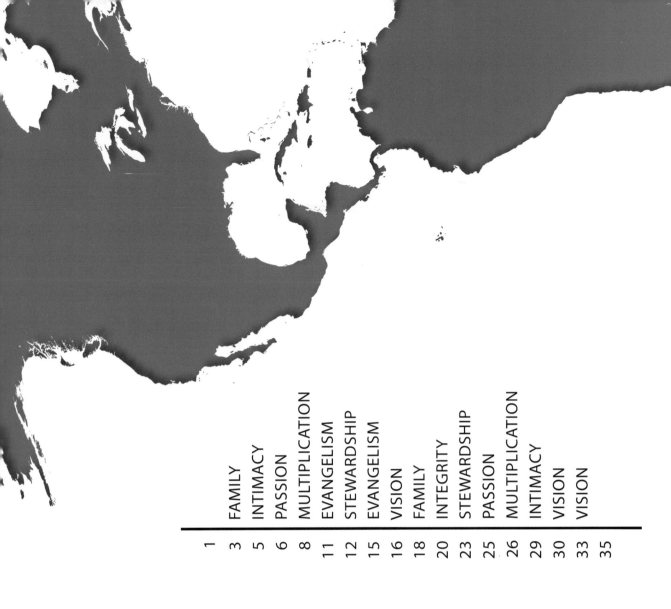

The Eight Core Values

Intimacy with God

God looks for consecrated men and women who lead out of an intimate relationship with God.

Passion for the Harvest

God looks for men and women who share a passion for those without Christ. Jesus came to "seek and to save the lost" (Luke 19:10). God desires that everyone be reached with the life-transforming power of the Gospel.

Visionary Leadership

God looks for men and women who are biblically committed to cast vision, set goals, mobilize the Body of Christ, and overcome obstacles in order to reach the nations for Christ.

Culturally Relevant Evangelism

God looks for men and women who live and teach the Gospel with cultural relevance, sensitivity, and power, so that the eternal truth of the Gospel will be understood and received in every culture of the world.

Multiplication of Leaders

God looks for men and women who disciple, coach, and mentor other leaders, who in turn become leaders of leaders who effectively train others.

Family Priority

God looks for men and women who are convinced that the family is God's building block for society and who make their family a priority in developing leaders.

Faithful Stewardship

God looks for men and women who are faithful stewards of finances, time, and spiritual gifts in their personal lives and leadership with the result that people are reached with the Gospel.

Integrity

God looks for men and women of integrity who live holy lives and who are accountable to God and to the Body of Christ. Integrity glorifies God, protects leaders from stumbling, and encourages growth.

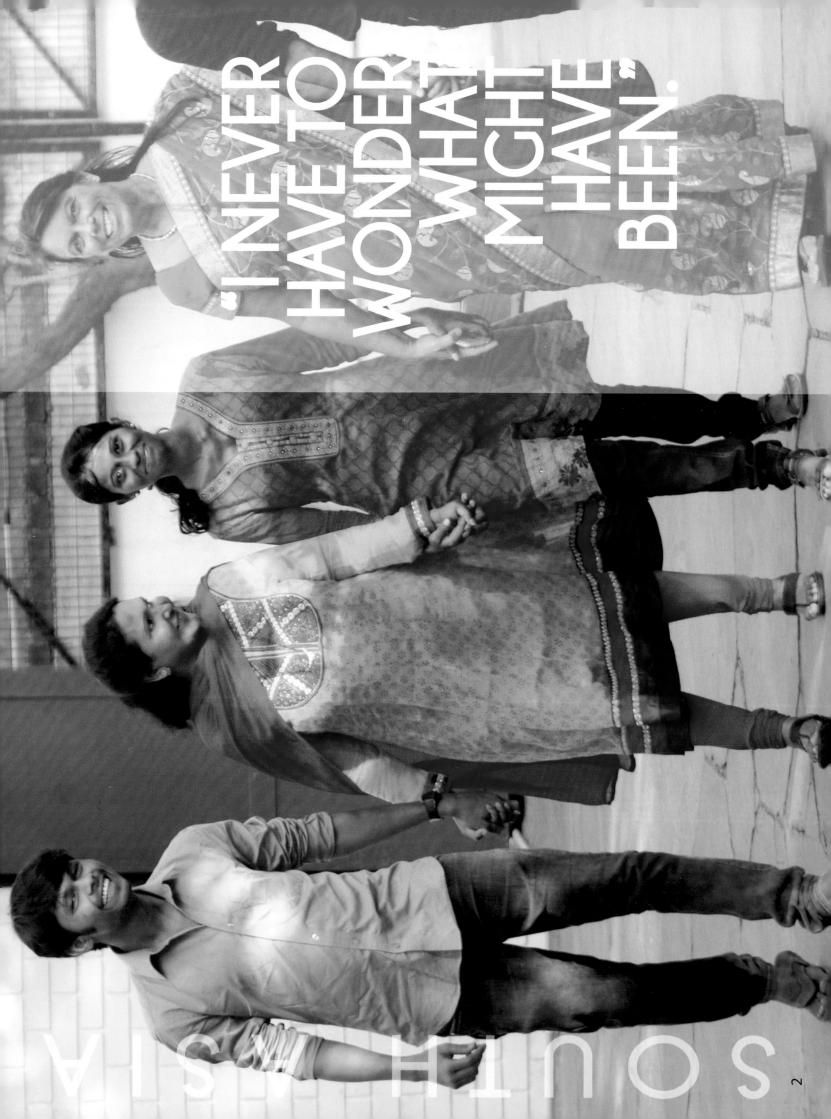

"I NEVER HAVE TO WONDER WHAT MIGHT HAVE BEEN."

India: Esther—You Must Be A Christian.

As we stepped into the back of the auto-rickshaw, the driver asked, "Where are you coming from?"

"We are coming from under the bridge," I replied.

Eyes wide, the driver turned around and said, "You must be a Christian. No one else would dare go down to those filthy street children."

His words replayed in my mind. There are nearly half a million street children in India, each with a tragic story, but all with the same result: abandoned, malnourished, uneducated, and often sleeping in a cardboard box or under a piece of plastic. At night, they rummage through the garbage in search of enough food just to survive. Girls are especially vulnerable.

I knew God was calling my husband, Peter, and me to trust Him and do more... but what? The taxi driver's comment increased my burden for these children. I cried out, "God, what do you want us to do? What does it mean for me to truly live as a Christian?"

Two years later, I sat witnessing God's answer to my cry. I gazed across the room at 63 beautiful children living in one of our Alpha Homes, laughing and calling out to us, "Mom! Dad!" One of those who became my daughter was Swapna. She tragically watched her mother die after a water truck pinned her against a wall. Swapna was just five years old at the time. Three years later, her father also passed away. Suddenly, she and her younger brother found themselves orphaned and alone. Heart broken by their story, Peter and I adopted them both.

Like all of my daughters, Swapna is special. She is an overcomer with a quick wit, a fierce devotion to her brother, and greatly loves Peter and me. She excelled in school and recently completed a bachelor degree with honors in nursing.

Sometimes I wonder, what if we had closed our eyes to the plight of the street children? What if we had not obeyed the vision? What if we had not trusted God? What if we had not defeated fear and dared to ask? I praise God that I never have to wonder what might have been.

Swapna is now a nurse who enjoys the attention of her parents, Peter and Esther Pereira. She gave her entire first salary to God's work. With her second paycheck, she bought her mother a new sari. Peter serves as the ILI International Director for South Asia. Watch Esther and Swapna's story at ILITeam.org/swapna.

FAMILY PRIORITY

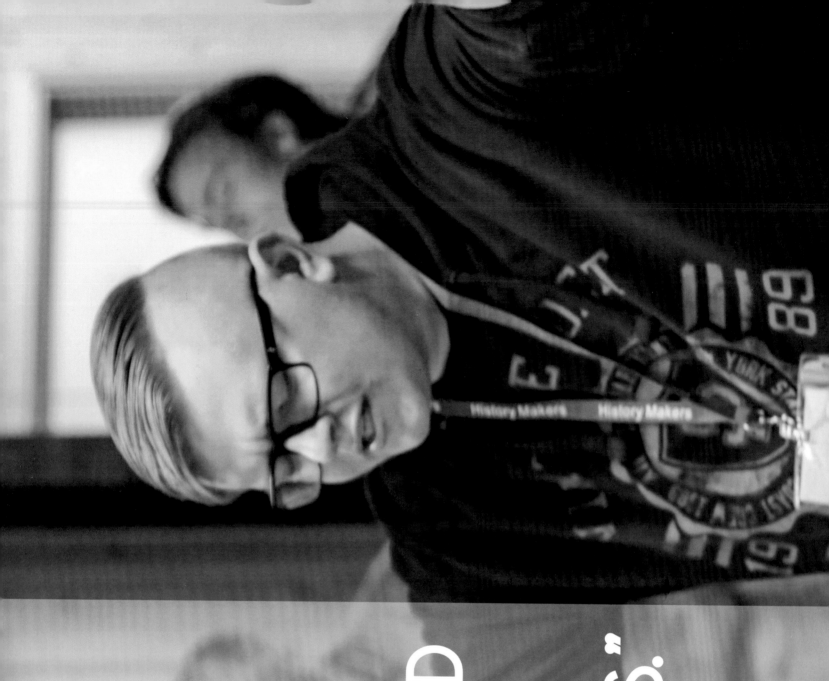

"I'M AN EX-DRUG ADDICT. JESUS, HE TURNED MY LIFE 180 DEGREES."

EUROPE

Iceland: Kjartan—Pure Gold. Iceland is a very dark place. Don't get me wrong, we have beautiful things, but spiritually… it gets really heavy. To fill the void, I turned to drugs and quickly became addicted.

For years, I was in real darkness. Addiction controlled my life. I was using drugs and hopelessly attempting to get sober. I could never truly grasp any clarity of mind. I was out of control and in a hopeless downward spiral. I wanted to change, but the drugs had control of my life.

All that changed when I encountered Jesus, the true source of life. When I drew close to Him, the heaviness was instantly gone, and I was set free. Now, I'm an ex-drug addict. Jesus, He turned my life 180 degrees. He gave me a new purpose for living, and it's pure gold.

I used to walk in darkness; now I walk in the light. I carry with me the mark of those who know their lives have been redeemed from the pit, who know they have been crowned with loving-kindness and compassion. This is what it means to have new life in Christ.

Now that I'm finally free, I want others to experience freedom too. I can't keep this to myself. My heart longs for others to have what has been given to me: **a chance to break free.**

> You are the light of the world. A town built on a hill cannot be hidden. Neither do people light a lamp and put it under a bowl. Instead they put it on its stand, and it gives light to everyone in the house. In the same way, let your light shine before others, that they may see your good deeds and glorify your Father in heaven.
> —Matthew 5:14-16

In 2015, Iceland held its first ILI History Makers Journey for young leaders, ages 20 to 35, to explore what it means to be an effective leader in their context. Joy Griffin and Martin Durham taught on the faculty. History Makers in Europe is led by Martin Durham, ILI International Director for Europe.

INTIMACY WITH GOD

Colombia: Weimar—We Go for Souls. "Pásalo! Pásalo! Pass it! Pass it!" The shouts of children sprinting across the soccer field joyfully filled the air and mingled with the birds of the Colombian forest around us. A few short dribbles and some fancy footwork, and the ball was off the ground, soaring into the back of the net.

A picture-perfect scene at the soccer ministry we put on for hundreds of kids, yet my mind races to a time when laughter and joy were unheard on this lush green field.

When I look at those kids kicking a soccer ball with such bliss, I can't help but see myself. Like most of them, I grew up without a father, surrounded by poverty and violence. For these kids, soccer is a desperate break from the abuse and fear that fills their homes—a chance to simply be children.

In Colombia, soccer is a way of life, but a cry deep within my heart constantly reminds me: *Soccer alone is not enough.* I vividly remember life without Jesus as my Savior, and I know just how desperately these kids need Him as well. They come to play ball, but we go for their souls.

The coaches run drills and scrimmages as they listen, guide, and love each child as though they were their own. Many of these children experience a sense of value, belonging, and acceptance for the first time in their lives. To a beautiful girl like Esperanza, a simple hug may seem like a meaningful gesture, but when I look into her eyes, I get a glimpse of the gravity of the embrace.

I am passionate about soccer but even more passionate about souls. When young boys and girls meet Jesus through soccer, their past is shed like dirty rags and a beautiful new story begins. I serve my risen Savior through the sport I love, and nothing touches my heart like seeing children meet Him for the first time on the field.

Weimar attended the 2013 Colombia National Conference led by Juan Bravo and the ILI Colombia Team. Weimar then began equipping more leaders in his nation, focusing on the younger generation through ILI's History Makers.

PASSION FOR THE HARVEST

"THEY COME TO PLAY BALL BUT WE GO FOR THEIR SOULS."

Malawi: Justin—Naked No More. I was naked when they found me. My world was hazy and terrifying. By day, I rooted through the garbage dump, eating what morsels I could find and hoping the sun would ward off my fear. By night, I trembled and screamed, scratching at my face to suppress the evil voices. I didn't know myself; I only knew the terrible darkness of the voices.

Then one day, I heard *new* voices. These people were not like me, they were clean and healthy. As I was scavenging through the trash, they came closer and lifted up their voices in prayers I had never heard. What prayers I had spoken before were feeble pleadings. These people spoke with boldness. I closed my eyes, darkness and fire twisted my vision. Screeches and screams filled my mind. My hands clawed at the waste around me and my stomach ached. Then all at once, the evil spirits and heavy dread were gone!

I blinked in the sunlight, unsure of the moment I just experienced. The people stood around me, commanding deliverance and speaking in the Name of a man named Jesus. They grew silent as I stood up, rising straighter than I had in 30 years. A man laughed and embraced me, and for the first time, I was not afraid.

The group walked me back to their venue and let me bathe. I stood beneath the falling water for the first time in years and felt the caked dirt, sweat, and waste melt from my arms and run in muddy swirls down the drain. With my filth flowed the darkness that had once possessed me. When I was finally clean, a woman brought me clothes, brand new clothes! Another man showed me how to button my shirt, and we chuckled at my clumsiness.

I walked with the others to my old home. It took a moment, but then a woman recognized me and began to shout, "Come and see!" Before long, hundreds of people were gathered around, touching my face and my hands, mouths open in wonder. They asked what changed in me, and my new friends shared with them the story of our Jesus. In the following days, many of them put their faith in the God who delivered me from the demons.

The men and women praying over Justin were History Makers (young, emerging leaders) who set aside time to evangelize in nearby towns during the week of their training in Malawi. The Malawi team is led by ILI International Director for English-Speaking Africa, David Thagana.

| MULTIPLICATION OF LEADERS

"ALL AT ONCE THE EVIL SPIRITS AND HEAVY DREAD WERE GONE!"

"THIS IS THE PLACE WHERE PEOPLE RECEIVE VISION."

CULTURALLY RELEVANT EVANGELISM

England: Kevin—Not Just the Leftovers. Before I knew it, I was standing in a room full of sight-impaired men and women physically embracing God's truth for the first time. Fingers slowly traced across the braille pages, some mouths silently forming the words as they read. I looked around the room and a thought occurred to me: *This is the place where people receive vision.*

As I spoke to these men and women, the first thing I saw was not their blindness, but that they are first and foremost God's children. I can't help but ask why the sight-impaired are too often cast into the margins of life. Why are the physically impaired often cast into the leftovers instead of being invited to the table?

When God prompted me to create an accessible version of *Christian to the Core** for the sight-impaired, I had no hesitation. Surely, the God who healed blindness could enable us to reach the blind with practical discipleship material. I often saw these believers confined to the second-hand knowledge of foundational discipleship truths, like listening to a lecture, but lacking the opportunities and resources for themselves.

Instead of merely listening to a presentation, these men and women would now be able to read for themselves, fully engage, and participate in the material. Inviting the visually impaired to the table is about much more than accessibility, it is about empowerment. As a friend of mine once said, "The Church should be the example of how we include every part of the Body of Christ."

Our vision is to see the teaching stretch beyond the material, multiplying as participants train others. These sight-impaired men and women are living into their callings as children of God with the confidence from holding God's Truth in their hands. They are now fully engaged in the disciple-making process in a new and exciting way.

Kevin worked with Torch Trust to publish braille and large-print versions of Christian to the Core for ministry to the sight-impaired. *Christian to the Core is ILI's discipleship resource based on the Eight Core Values.

11

Myanmar: Leik—Offering Everything. Irene rushed into the room. "Pastor Leik, Did you hear? The death count is estimated at nearly 100—My hometown, my friends, my family, they're…"

A solemn silence pierced the room… "What are you doing?"

"Writing an email," I answered. "We will need prayer."

To the ILI Asia Pacific Team, I trust you are praying for us and the nation of Myanmar. We are preparing to leave for Chin State soon. Our friends are waiting on us to help provide relief for those affected by the devastating floods. God has called, and we simply can't stay here anymore. My heart is already there, and our team is prepared to go as God leads. Please join us in prayer. Together, we can stand in the gap for the weak and needy.

In great distress, I sent the email and opened my Bible to Isaiah 6:8, "Here am I. Send me." I knelt to the ground and began to pray fervently, "Send me Lord… I will go, send me. Send me." I repeated the plea well into the night. Then, God answered our prayers.

Pastor Leik, thank you for contacting us. Because of your email, we mobilized the ILI Asia Pacific leaders and raised prayer and financial support to help your team go and aid the flood victims. We are one team. Together, we can share the love of Christ and provide relief.

"Irene, pack your things! Our God has delivered! The supplies… a team… God has provided everything we need. We must share with those in need that our God will provide for them, too." Scaling the sides of mountains and hauling heavy bags of food, we pressed on to reach the lost and hurting. When we were tired and sore, God's resounding truth flooded my mind… "I will not offer to God that which cost me nothing" (2 Sam. 24:24). We had to be faithful stewards with all God had entrusted to us.

From village to village, the Lord was with us. The many faces of those we encountered resembled the face of Christ. I heard Jesus say, "For I was hungry and you gave me something to eat, I was thirsty and you gave me something to drink, I was a stranger and you invited me in"(Matt. 25:35).

Pastor Leik graduated from an ILI training event in January 2015. She now helps lead ILI training in Myanmar with the Asia Pacific Team, led by ILI International Director for Asia Pacific, John Lim.

FAITH-FUL **STEWARDSHIP**

"I WILL NOT OFFER TO GOD THAT WHICH COST ME NOTHING."

ASIA PACIFIC

"TODAY WE LEAVE CHANGED READY TO FORGIVE THOSE WHO KILLED OUR LOVED ONES."

14

CULTURALLY RELEVANT EVANGELISM

Nigeria: Jerry—Forgiving Terrorists. For four days, my heart sank and my stomach churned as I sat in a room filled with 100 women—all freshly widowed. They were scared, angry, sad, and traumatized because of the horrific means by which Boko Haram terrorized their families. For many, their husbands and children were beaten, tortured, kidnapped, and even killed, sometimes before their very own eyes. One woman developed a deep, psychological problem after being forced to sit and watch Boko Haram terrorists slaughter her husband and seven boys.

A gut-wrenching sickness overtook my body; never in my life had I been up-close to stories such as these. When I first learned of these gruesome events, my heart leapt from my chest to act quickly. Something had to be done, but what? That's when God made His plan known. Just as clouds parting after a terrifying storm, God spoke and revealed to me what these women needed most in a single word… **Healing.** So we set out to do just that.

One by one, the women poured out their hearts, cried, and slowly began the journey of healing and recovery. They came to the altar, wrote their struggles, bitterness, anger, and laid them at the foot of the cross, weeping and clinging to a small piece of paper. We shared the Gospel and explained Christ's unconditional love and forgiveness, and we taught them how we are called to forgive our persecutors, just as Jesus forgave our sins. Professional counselors ministered to them day after day.

"How can we forgive those who have done this brutal and sadistic evil to us?" One woman asked. Before I could answer, she continued, "But since you taught us that God expects us to forgive and love those who have offended us, we will obey Him and do so."

Another woman approached me and said, "When we came for trauma healing, our hearts were heavy, bitter, and vengeful, but today, we are leaving changed, ready to forgive those who have tortured and killed our loved ones."

Most people think miraculous healing looks like the blind seeing, the deaf hearing, and the lame walking, but sometimes, miraculous healing looks like widows and grieving mothers forgiving the murderers of their loved ones.

Jerry traveled from Nigeria to be equipped at the 2008 Zambia History Makers Journey. He now serves on the faculty of many ILI and History Makers events each year. He is a true champion for the ILI Global Team and the spread of the Gospel in Africa.

Cuba: Maria—From Cuba to the Middle East. "Maria, come stand next to me."

I was not prepared to hear those words from Tony Vasquez as he was preaching on the Great Commission at my church to nearly 800 women in Havana, Cuba. I was sitting on the platform behind him with the other pastors.

He turned and smiled at me and said, "Maria, yes, come quickly!"

As I walked forward, he reached beneath his Bible on the pulpit and pulled out a large cloth map of the world. He unfolded it and looked back to the congregation, "As you all know, God has called Maria to be a missionary from Cuba to the Middle East. Although you are a 4,000-member church, you have never sent a missionary from this congregation, and she has a call from God on her life!"

Tony held up the cloth for everyone to see the map of the world. Then, he wrapped the cloth around my shoulders. My heart was racing as I heard him say, "Maria, God has called you. Now is the time for us to pray for God to open the door so you can go. Go stand in the middle of the aisle so the women can lay hands on you and pray."

I walked to the center of the church wearing the map of the world like a shawl. I felt the hands of my sisters on my shoulders as the entire sanctuary erupted in prayer.

The next morning, I met with Tony and ILI President, Wes Griffin. I looked them in the eyes with deep conviction and said, "I am a Cuban woman. I know how to live on nothing. God has called me, and I will go to the Middle East to share Jesus with Muslim women and lead them to Christ."

One week later, God opened the door, and soon I will be sharing Christ with women in a closed nation in the Middle East.

Maria is an ILI Cuba alumni under the leadership of Tony Vasquez, ILI International Director for Latin America. She accepted the call to be a missionary in the Middle East where she plans to lead women to Christ.

VISIONARY LEADER-
SHIP

"GOD HAS CALLED ME TO THE MIDDLE EAST TO SHARE JESUS WITH MUSLIM WOMEN."

LATIN AMERICA

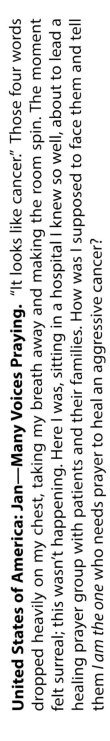

United States of America: Jan—Many Voices Praying. "It looks like cancer." Those four words dropped heavily on my chest, taking my breath away and making the room spin. The moment felt surreal; this wasn't happening. Here I was, sitting in a hospital I knew so well, about to lead a healing prayer group with patients and their families. How was I supposed to face them and tell them *I am the one who needs prayer to heal an aggressive cancer?*

Immediately, I emailed Wes and Joy Griffin at ILI, unsure of what to say. Wes quickly called me on the phone. With a slight tremble in my voice, I shared the news and asked for prayer. I have seen God work, and I know He has the power to heal me; my responsibility is to ask. Not long after my conversation with Wes, a flood of emails, messages, and phone calls full of encouragement and love began pouring into my inbox from all over the world—my faithful brothers and sisters were on their knees in prayer on my behalf.

The ILI global family had been mobilized. The voices from dozens of international leaders were lifted up in agreement: "Lord, heal Jan." They trusted God, but braced for the worst.

With each precious note from ILI leaders around the world, my spirit, soul, and body were washed in the love of Jesus. A malignant lump was quietly growing in my lower abdomen, but I clung to a Savior who died for me and the prayers of fellow believers lifting my name.

The doctors expected a long, complex surgery with an even more difficult period of follow-up treatment. Yet God had greater plans in store. The operation only lasted two hours, and the doctors saw no need for further treatments. The tumor was entirely contained! The ILI leaders dared to ask God for healing, and He answered in a huge way. I am now a living testimony to other patients about the healing love of God and seeds of hope being scattered here and abroad.

Sometimes, reaching the nations for Christ means going to places we don't wish to go—even hospitals; but, He goes with us, testifying to His glory as we yield our bodies as living sacrifices. He is, after all, the Great Physician.

Jan first experienced ILI through an introductory seminar in 2010. Later that year, she served on the faculty of a National Conference in Brazil. Now she serves as faculty in several ILI conferences around the world each year.

|FAMILY PRIOR-
RITY

"SOMETIMES REACHING THE NATIONS FOR CHRIST MEANS GOING PLACES WE DON'T WANT TO GO—EVEN HOSPITALS."

NORTH AMERICA

Zambia: Alfred—The President's Funeral. My eyes scanned the 50,000 people on Parliament grounds. Hundreds of thousands more were watching the broadcast live on national television. Large screens were placed in cities throughout the nation for public viewing of the funeral of Zambian, President Michael Chilufya Sata.

I took one last deep breath and walked to the microphone to preach the president's funeral and proclaim the hope of the Gospel to my grieving nation. Numerous African heads of state and other international diplomats, government officials, members of Parliament, cabinet members, and the first Zambian president, Kenneth Kaunda, were in attendance.

As a boy, I never could have imagined being selected for this honor. Raised in a remote village in a polygamist family, my father had three wives, and we worshipped animistic gods. Living in poverty, I never wore shoes until the age of fifteen. I thought if there was a God and He loved me, my circumstances would have been different, and my parents would not have divorced. I saw education as my way out of poverty so I excelled in school, eventually landing a cherished spot in a missionary school in Choma. Bitter, stubborn, and unbelieving, I disliked the missionaries, but I wanted the education they offered.

In my third year, a missionary was teaching on Revelation 3:20 and said, "Jesus does not force Himself on you, but if you open the door of your heart, He will come in." He continued, "Some of you think God doesn't love you, but I want to tell you God loves you just as you are." I felt Jesus gently knocking at the door of my heart. Later that night, I knelt and said, "God if you are real, I need you right now."

As I concluded the sermon for President Sata's funeral, I proclaimed, "Death is certain. No one is exempt: rich or poor, powerful or weak. No profession is exempt, from diplomats to the common person on the street. I challenge you today to choose Christ so you can spend eternity in heaven with Him. May the death of our president be a clear wake up call for everyone to accept Jesus Christ, who has conquered death!"

Alfred and Muumbe Kalembo attended the 2003 ILI International Conference. Alfred was the first pastor in his denomination to receive a Master of Divinity and Doctor of Ministry degrees. Today, he is the National Superintendent of the Pilgrim Wesleyan Church of Zambia as well as the President of the Zambia National Council of Churches.

| INTEGRITY

"MAY THE DEATH OF OUR PRESIDENT BE A CLEAR WAKE UP CALL TO ACCEPT JESUS CHRIST!"

SOUTHERN AFRICA

"I ASKED GOD, 'WHY ARE YOU DOING THIS?'"

Thailand: John Lim—From the Rising of the Sun. I never miss the Chinese New Year season in Singapore. The festive and vibrant three-day event is always a highlight for our family. So when I was invited to attend the ILI International Conference in Nairobi, Kenya during that time, I hesitated. Still, I prayed and clearly heard God say, "Go." So I obeyed.

During the conference, God spoke to me about spreading the Gospel, reminding me that by His blood, Jesus "purchased for God persons from every tribe and language and people and nation" (Rev. 5:9).

Paul Low, another Singaporean businessman, and I were already preaching the Gospel in Thailand, but everything changed that week as God poured a fresh passion for the lost into our hearts. We invited other lay people to join us. This was our opportunity to be good stewards of the time, finances, and spiritual gifts God entrusted to us.

We would run our businesses in Singapore during the week and fly to Thailand on the weekend to preach the Gospel, equip leaders, and plant churches. We began by focusing on villages with no churches. God performed miracles by healing the sick, delivering the oppressed, and saving all who called on His Name. We saw farmers, hawkers, construction workers, and business people from different languages and dialects come to Christ. We preached in refugee camps on the borders. We traveled from the tops of mountains to depths of valleys.

Men, women, and children were responding! Then we received a call from Myanmar, similar to the Macedonian call in the Bible, "Come and help us." So we went. Then came the call from India, then Bhutan, then Cambodia...

I asked God, "Why are you doing this?" And He showed me Isaiah 45:5-6.

> *I am the Lord, and there is no other; apart from Me there is no God. I will strengthen you . . . so that from the rising of the sun to the place of its setting people may know there is none besides Me. I am the LORD, and there is no other.*

Then it dawned on me. God was extending our reach from east to west, from the rising to the setting sun, preaching the Good News so people would know there is none but Him.

John Lim and Paul Low, along with a team of lay people in the Asia Pacific region, are responsible for training more than 7,000 people in the last 10 years. John attended the 2006 Nairobi International Conference in Kenya and trained Paul at the 2008 Bangkok National Conference in Thailand.

"IF WE DON'T MAKE OUR HISTORY, WHO WILL?"

Iraq: Yousef—Responding to God's Call.

The air was heavy and reeked of trash and foul odors. As we made our way through the refugee camp with hundreds of bags of food and supplies, a little boy in worn and dirty clothes looked up at me with pain-filled, hungry eyes.

"What's your name?" I asked.

"Sami."

"Are you hungry, Sami?"

He nodded and told me his family didn't eat dinner most nights because they have no food. "Sometimes we get to eat bread," he said, "but most of the time we just boil and eat grass cut from the fields." My heart sank deep. With great concern, we brought Sami's family a bag of food and prayed over them. Word spread quickly throughout the camp that we were distributing food. Much to our surprise, the refugees' immediate request was for something other than food. They tightly grasped our hands, looked intently into our eyes, and simply asked for prayer.

We knew their pain was deeper than physical hunger, their souls were desperate for much more. They were crying out for a Savior. Listening to story after story of heartbreak, horror, and pain, we carefully assured them that God sees and cares for them. We shared the hope of the Gospel, and many eagerly accepted Jesus into their lives that day. We left the camp with great confidence, fully aware God was moving among those refugees.

After helping with the relief project, we held a History Makers Journey for emerging leaders. One of the participants, deeply impacted by our time in the refugee camp, stood before the group and asked, "If we don't make our history, who will?" Before anyone could speak, he answered with genuine conviction, "I think we must make history ourselves, or others will make it for us in the wrong way."

Jesus does not call us to live comfortably, He calls us to "Go and make disciples of all nations." Our responsibility is to bring the Kingdom everywhere we set foot.

Yousef is ILI's International Director for the Middle East-North Africa. The History Makers participants made a decision to provide relief effort just before the conference began at a nearby refugee camp. There were 35 participants including Syrians, Kurds, Yazidis, and Iraqis from both Muslim Background Believers (MBBs) and Christian Background Believers (CBBs).

PASSION FOR THE HARVEST

India: Ashwin—Jesus the Healer. I was running out of ideas. Suffering from a strange, long-term illness, I visited countless doctors in the region and spent more than I could truly afford in hopes of someone bringing me back to health. Not a single medical professional could identify this illness—I was no closer to being well than when I began the search for healing. Desperate and in pain, I resorted to witch doctors in search of a cure, to no avail.

Finally, a friend told me of a Christian pastor in the area who could possibly provide help. I reached out, desperate to find restoration, and the pastor agreed to meet. He listened as I described my illness and the great lengths I had gone in hopes of being healed. As I finished, the pastor looked at me with hope-filled eyes, silently conveying he had the answer I was in search of. He explained to me the God who created me also had the power to heal me, "If we believe in the Lord Jesus, He will surely heal us."

In that life-defining moment, I decided to throw away all doubt and hesitation overshadowing my heart and put my complete hope in Jesus. I closed my eyes as the pastor prayed. Instantly, I was healed! Gone were the mysterious symptoms, the pain, and the fear. The Great Physician did what no other doctor was able to do!

I accepted Jesus as my personal Savior and began attending church services where I learned of God's love. As I studied Scripture, I realized the truth within my Bible was much too important for me to keep to myself. The desire to share my knowledge and love of the God who heals grew more intense as God took me deeper in intimacy with Him.

I set to work and started a house church. Before long, 20 people were meeting weekly to learn about sin, forgiveness, and the risen Christ. Then, we planted a second house church in another region. By the grace of God, believers are now growing day by day. My heart's desire is to serve the Body of Christ in Jesus' Name. I praise God because this man who was once desperate to be healed is now the shepherd to many believers.

Ashwin was equipped at the 2015 India National Conference led by ILI International Director for South Asia, Peter Pereira. Ashwin is dedicated to seeing more churches planted and the Gospel spread in his region.

MULTIPLICATION OF LEADERS

"THE TRUTH WITHIN THOSE PAGES WAS TOO MUCH TOO IMPORTANT FOR ME TO KEEP TO MYSELF."

"I COULD NEVER GIVE UP ON JESUS, HE'S TOO DEEP INSIDE OF ME."

Eritrea: Paulos—Refugee Redemption. After hours of questioning and physical abuse, the soldier yelled out once again, "Deny this Jesus as your Savior, and you will go free."

A faint and simple response fell from my lips, "No."

The blows of his fists and kicks were excruciating. Grinning as though he had figured a way to keep me from sharing my faith, the sergeant said, "If you promise to never meet with other Christians, you may leave here today."

My head pounding and my body aching, I unapologetically responded, "I cannot make that promise. Christians always meet together." They dragged me outside, threw me into the back of a truck, and drove for a long time. Finally stopping, there was complete silence, just a faint wind and the almost unbearable heat remained. My cell was a shipping container in the middle of the desert. The soldier shoved me inside and secured the lock. I had no idea when or if he would ever come back. Suddenly, the grim reality sank in: I was going die in this container.

The next day, a soldier returned with a cup of lentil soup, some bread, and a cup of tea. Day after day for the next year, this was the routine. The pain in my stomach became agonizing. I was so weak I could no longer sit up on my own. Shockingly, the sergeant released me to go home as he saw my death nearing.

But God had other plans; for the next two years, I laid in bed and became stronger. Eventually, I gained enough strength and confidence to escape Eritrea. I planned my route through the mine fields guarded by soldiers who were given the order to "shoot and kill" anyone attempting to flee. It was my only option for freedom. By God's grace, I made it to a refugee camp in Northern Sudan.

As I finished sharing my story with Al, he sat in silence for a few moments, eyes fixated on something in the distance. Finally, processing the brutal realities, he looked at me and asked, "What did Jesus ever do for you? You lost your family, your country, and almost your life. Why didn't you give up on Jesus?"

"Oh, I could never give up on Jesus," I replied. "He is too deep inside of me. In a moment of tremendous pain, I cried out to Him, 'Jesus, I need to touch you.' With full assurance, I heard Him say, 'You don't need to reach out and touch Me. I am holding you.' Because Jesus never gave up on me, I will never give up on Him."

Paulos attended the National Conference in Sudan for Eritrean refugees, where 30 men and women were equipped to spread the Gospel. Al Vom Steeg, ILI Senior International Director, served alongside the national faculty to teach and mentor participants.

INTIMACY WITH GOD

Pakistan: Samira—Dangerous Women. I nervously pushed my way through the crowd in route to the ILI Regional Conference. Suddenly, something horrific caught my attention. There, on the ground in the middle of the city was a woman... dead, stoned to death by her father and brother for refusing to marry the man of their choice. I took a deep breath and pushed back tears of anger and deep anguish.

The government does nothing to stop these "mercy killings." Law enforcement even allows bloody, lifeless bodies to lie in the street as an example for other women. In a nation 97% Muslim and ruled by Sharia Law, Christian persecution runs high and women continue to struggle with fewer rights than men.

Traveling that day as a Pakistani woman to a Christian leadership conference, I was well aware of the danger I was putting my life in. Fighting the paralysis of fear, the voice of the Holy Spirit filled my mind and drowned the noise of doubt. Relief washed over me as I finally arrived at the conference. I was welcomed by the bright smiles of women eagerly awaiting their opportunity for leadership training.

The room was full, 61 women from different regions of Pakistan. Just being here put them, as well as their family and friends, at great risk. Then I found a familiar face, ILI International Director, Sister Joy Griffin. A few weeks prior, Joy was denied a visa on claims of being "spiritually dangerous" to Pakistan—a true compliment! Many of the women fasted and prayed, and the visa was granted. This is when I first heard the Holy Spirit whisper, "Unstoppable."

During the conference, I was deeply challenged by Acts 4, where Peter and John are heavily persecuted for proclaiming the message of Jesus, but they continue to preach boldly. This time, the word slipped out of my mouth, "Unstoppable!" I felt heads turn toward me with eyes wide in excitement. The women all nodded and agreed, "The Gospel is unstoppable!" We may be Pakistani, Christian women, but we are determined to be dangerous women for Christ. The message of the Gospel is *unstoppable.*

Samira and the other 60 women who attended the Pakistan Regional Conference trained over 1,000 leaders in various regions within 7 months of their training. Bishop Yaqub Paul is the ILI Director for Pakistan and has a heart to see Pakistani, Christian women trained and raised up to make an impact across their nation.

VISIONARY LEADER-SHIP

"WE MAY BE PAKISTANI, CHRISTIAN WOMEN, BUT WE ARE DETERMINED TO BE DANGEROUS FOR CHRIST."

"I HAD A BURNING PASSION WAITING TO BE RELEASED THROUGH GOD'S VISION FOR MY LIFE"

EUROPE - AFRICA

32

Kenya and Switzerland: Rebekka—The Narrow Path. I chose the narrow path. I chose to walk by faith and not by sight, following the sound of God's voice. In the back of my mind, I could hear the skeptics telling me I was too young to see such an ambitious vision come to life. Still, I have learned when my dreams are seemingly too big for this world, God can do "immeasurably more than all we ask or imagine, according to His power that is at work within us" (Eph. 3:20).

Five years ago, when I traveled from Switzerland to Kenya for an internship at the Tumaini Children's Home, I was invited to attend the Kenya History Makers Journey. During one of the sessions, I heard the words that immediately reached deep inside my soul,

"Passion is a burning force within, seizing you with a power to move beyond ordinary human activity. It won't let you go until God's goals are reached."

It was as though the facilitator was speaking directly to me, as if he knew I had this burning passion waiting to be released through God's vision for my life. I immediately had a deeper connection to God's heart for the least and the lost.

That week, God birthed a vision in me, which changed my life and the lives of many others forever. My heart was set on caring for the least of these in Kenya and raising up a generation of young leaders in Switzerland and Kenya. I imagined an organization that would feed, educate, and provide clothing for orphaned children in Kenya. Although I was unsure how to see this vision fulfilled, I was willing to trust and dare to ask God for a way. I also knew I had to find a way to see History Makers established back in my homeland of Switzerland.

Today, I lead an organization empowering leaders, impacting the lives of many children in Kenya, and enabling a volunteer program for Swiss youth and young adults. I am fully committed to the role of a History Maker to equip leaders and spread the Gospel in Kenya, Switzerland, and beyond!

Rebekka attended the Kenya History Makers Journey in 2011. The non-profit organization she envisioned during her training now impacts the lives of over 400 children in Kenya and facilitates a volunteer program for Swiss youth, bringing 30-40 volunteers to Kenya annually. She and her team also launched History Makers in Switzerland.

VISIONARY LEADER-SHIP

DARE *to* ASK

THANK YOU

We want to take this opportunity to thank everyone who made this book possible. The journeys of the men, women, youth, and children impacted by the ILI Team are countless, and we pray God's story of redemption and mercy is evident on each page.

The ILI leadership team and alumni around the world are dedicated to multiplying their training into the lives of others in order to effectively spread the transforming power of the Gospel. Each of those leaders are a great inspiration, and this book is dedicated to them.

Finally, ILI's global impact and ability to continue equipping leaders and spreading the Gospel worldwide would be impossible without the prayers and financial support of our faithful partners. We pray these stories have inspired you and provide a tangible example of how ILI's partners are fulfilling Christ's command to "go and make disciples" (Matt. 28:19-20).

Learn More about the International Leadership Institute. To learn more about ILI and our globally recognized leadership curriculum, visit ILITeam.org. To explore ILI's global initiative for young leaders, visit History-Makers.org. To learn more about ILI's discipleship resource, Christian to the Core, visit ChristiantotheCore.org.